WORDS

OF THE

PROPHET MUḤAMMAD

صلى الله عليه وسلم

SELECTIONS FROM THE ḤADĪTH

COMPILED BY

MAULANA WAHIDUDDIN KHAN

Other books by Maulana Wahiduddin Khan

God Arises:
The Evidence of God in Nature and in Science

Woman between Islam and Western Society

God-Oriented Life

Muhammad: The Prophet of Revolution

Islam As It Is

Islam: The Voice of Human Nature

Islam: Creator of the Modern Age

Religion and Science

Indian Muslims: The Need For A Positive Outlook

Woman in Islamic Shari'ah

Tabligh Movement

Tazkirul Qur'an
(Commentary of the Qur'an, in 2 volumes)

Allahu Akbar
(God is Great, in Urdu)

Al-Islam Yatahadda
(Modern Challenges to Islam, in Arabic)

The publisher would like to thank the following persons who made this book possible:

Wg. Cdr. M. Yusuf Khan
Anna Khanna
Farida Khanam
Susan Brady Maitra
Saniyasnain Khan
Anis Luqman Nadvi

ISBN 81-85063-08-7

First published 1996

Urdu/Arabic version: *Hadith-e-Rasul*

Al-Risala Books
The Islamic Centre
1, Nizamuddin West Market, New Delhi 110 013
Tel. 4611128, Fax: 91-11-4697333

Distributed in U.K. by

Assalaam International Ltd.
481, Coventry Road, Birmingham B10 0JS
Tel. 0121-773 7117, Fax: 0121-773 7771

Distributed in U.S.A. by

Maktaba Al-Risala
1439 Ocean Ave., 4C Brooklyn, New York NY 11230
Tel. 718-2583435

Foreword

The present volume is an anthology compiled from the Ḥadīth literature, an Islamic source second only to the Qur'ān in religious importance. Although brief, it covers, directly or indirectly, the more important aspects of the Ḥadīth's teachings. The sayings of the Prophet Muḥammad ﷺ have been handed down to posterity through both oral and written traditions, the foundations of which were laid by the Prophet's Companions, some of whom were also his scribes.

The following are some of the principles by which he sought to guide his followers. Eternal in essence, they are of value not only to Muslims, but to humanity at large.

— 1 —

Islam has been built on five pillars:
testifying that there is no god but Allah
and Muḥammad is His Messenger;
performance of prayers;
alms-giving (*zakāt*);
pilgrimage to the Kaʿbah;
fasting during Ramaḍān.

ḤADĪTH OF AL-BUKHĀRĪ AND MUSLIM
ON THE AUTHORITY OF ʿABDULLĀH IBN ʿUMAR.

— 2 —

Anyone who befriends another
or makes an enemy,
gives or withholds,
has perfected his faith,
if what he does is done for the sake of
the Almighty.

ḤADĪTH OF AL-BUKHĀRĪ
ON THE AUTHORITY OF ABŪ UMĀMAH.

— 3 —

When the Prophet Muḥammad ﷺ was asked by ʿAmr ibn ʿAbasah what was meant by faith, he replied, 'Self-restraint and gentleness.'

ḤADĪTH OF MUSLIM.

— 4 —

One who is willing to accept
God as his Lord,
Islam as his religion
and Muḥammad as God's Messenger
has savoured the taste of faith.

ḤADĪTH OF AL-BUKHĀRĪ AND MUSLIM ON THE AUTHORITY OF AL-ʿABBĀS IBN ʿABD AL-MUṬṬALIB.

— 5 —

Simplicity, too, is a part of faith.

ḤADĪTH OF ABŪ DĀWŪD
ON THE AUTHORITY OF ABŪ UMĀMAH.

— 6 —

A man without trust
is a man without faith.
And a man who does not fulfill his
promises is a man without faith.

ḤADĪTH OF AḤMAD IBN ḤANBAL.
ON THE AUTHORITY OF ANAS IBN MĀLIK.

— 7 —

Greed and faith can never co-exist
in the human heart.

ḤADĪTH OF AN-NASĀ'Ī
ON THE AUTHORITY OF ABŪ HURAYRAH.

— 8 —

God loves those believers who labour to
earn a living through lawful means.

ḤADĪTH OF AT-TABARĀNĪ
ON THE AUTHORITY OF ʿABDULLĀH IBN ʿUMAR.

— 9 —

Actions are judged by their intention
and every man shall be judged
accordingly.
Thus he whose migration was for Allah
and His Messenger; his migration was
for Allah and His Messenger;
and he whose migration was to achieve
some worldly benefit or to take some
women in marriage, his migration was
for that for which he migrated.

ḤADĪTH OF AL-BUKHĀRĪ AND MUSLIM
ON THE AUTHORITY OF ʿUMAR IBN AL-KHAṬṬĀB.

— 10 —

When you see sycophants, throw dust in
their faces.

ḤADĪTH OF MUSLIM
ON THE AUTHORITY OF MIQDĀD IBN ASWAD.

— 11 —

Asked what reward there would be for a man who desired fame and compensation for having performed *jihād*, the Prophet said, 'there is no reward for him.' When asked the same question three times over, the Prophet gave the same reply each time. Then he said, 'God accepts those deeds which were performed purely for His sake and which were meant to seek His pleasure.'

ḤADĪTH OF ABŪ DĀWŪD AND AN-NASĀ'Ī ON THE AUTHORITY OF ABŪ UMĀMAH.

— 12 —

Keep your faith pure.
Even the smallest good deed will suffice.

ACCORDING TO AL-MUNDHIRĪ WHEN MUʿADH IBN JABAL WAS APPOINTED RULER OF YEMEN, HE ASKED THE PROPHET FOR ADVICE AND WAS GIVEN THE ABOVE REPLY.

— 13 —

One who says his prayers (*ṣalāt*) with
great propriety when he is in the
presence of others,
but does so without proper reverence
when he is alone,
is committing an act of contempt
for his Lord.

ḤADĪTH OF AL-MUNDHIRĪ
ON THE AUTHORITY OF ʿABDULLĀH IBN MASʿŪD.

— 14 —

When a person repents,
God's pleasure at this is even greater
than that of one who dismounts from
his camel, loses it in the desert and then
finds it again all of a sudden.

ḤADĪTH OF AL-BUKHĀRĪ AND MUSLIM
ON THE AUTHORITY OF ANAS IBN MĀLIK.

—15—

According to ʿAmr ibn al-ʿĀṣ, the Prophet Muḥammad ﷺ sent word to him to come clad in armour and bearing arms. 'When I came into his presence, he was performing his ablutions.' The Prophet said to me, 'O ʿAmr, I am sending you on a mission. God will bring you back safe and will reward you with spoils.' I said, 'O Prophet, I did not migrate for the spoils. It was for the sake of God and His Messenger.' The Prophet replied, 'The best wealth for a good man to possess is that which has been lawfully acquired.'

ḤADĪTH OF AḤMAD IBN ḤANBAL.

— 16 —

None of you truly believes until your own inclinations are in accordance with the message I have brought.

ḤADĪTH QUOTED BY
AN-NAWAWĪ FROM *KITĀB AL-HUJJAH*
ON THE AUTHORITY OF ʿABDULLĀH IBN ʿAMR IBN AL-ʿĀṢ

— 17 —

God has imposed certain moral
obligations, do not abrogate them;
He has forbidden certain things,
do not indulge in them;
He has laid down certain limits,
do not transgress them;
He is silent on certain matters,
do not knowingly argue over them.

ḤADĪTH OF AD-DARQUTNĪ
ON THE AUTHORITY OF ABŪ THAʿLABAH.

— 18 —

There is a covenant of *ṣalāt* (prayers)
between me and the people.
Therefore, if a man gives up *ṣalāt*,
he is guilty of *kufr* (infidelity).

ḤADĪTH OF AḤMAD, AT-TIRMIDHĪ, AN-NASĀ'Ī AND IBN MĀJAH ON THE AUTHORITY OF BURAYDAH.

— 19 —

ʿUmar ibn al-Khaṭṭāb wrote to his
governors that the most important thing
of all to him was prayer (*ṣalāt*).
A man who prayed regularly
safeguarded his faith.
And a man who was found wanting in
his prayers would be found wanting
even more in other matters.

MISHKĀT AL-MAṢĀBĪḤ.

— 20 —

A *ṣalāt* offered in congregation
is 27 times more worthy of reward than
the *ṣalāt* offered
alone.

ḤADĪTH OF AL-BUKHĀRĪ AND MUSLIM
ON THE AUTHORITY OF ʿABDULLĀH IBN ʿUMAR.

— 21 —

Anywhere that three Muslims reside,
the prayer must be offered in
congregation, otherwise Satan will
overpower them.
Adhere, therefore, to congregational
prayer, lest the wolf eat up the goat
which strays away from the herd.

ḤADĪTH BY ABŪ DĀWŪD
ON THE AUTHORITY OF ABŪʾD-DARDĀ.

— 22 —

When you lead the prayer,
you should make it short
because, among those offering *ṣalāt* there
may be some who are
infirm, sick and old.
But when you offer individual prayers,
you may lengthen them as much
as you wish.

ḤADĪTH OF AL-BUKHĀRĪ
ON THE AUTHORITY OF ABŪ HURAYRAH.

— 23 —

When I stand for *ṣalāt*,
I want to offer a long prayer,
but I shorten it when I hear a child's
cry, because I do not want to cause
anxiety to the mother.

ḤADĪTH OF AL-BUKHĀRĪ
ON THE AUTHORITY OF ABŪ QATĀDAH.

— 24 —

Jābir ibn Samurah related how he used to offer Friday prayers with the Prophet. He said that the latter's prayer, as well as his sermon were moderate in length.

ḤADĪTH OF MUSLIM.

— 25 —

Everything has a cleansing agent. And fasting is the cleansing agent for the body. Fasting is more a matter of patience than of anything else.

ḤADĪTH OF IBN MĀJAH ON THE AUTHORITY OF ABŪ HURAYRAH.

— 26 —

If the observer of a fast does not give up
false utterances and their pursuit,
then God does not require him to give
up his food and water.

ḤADĪTH OF AL-BUKHĀRĪ AND MUSLIM
ON THE AUTHORITY OF ABŪ HURAYRAH.

— 27 —

Fasting is like a shield.
When one of you is observing a fast,
neither should you indulge in indecent
talk nor should you create an uproar.
And if someone talks ill of you,
or fights with you,
you should just say,
'I am observing my fast.'

ḤADĪTH OF AL-BUKHĀRĪ AND MUSLIM
ON THE AUTHORITY OF ABŪ HURAYRAH.

— 28 —

The man who keeps a fast in full faith,
and for reward in the world hereafter,
will be forgiven his past sins.
And the man who prays in the night
during Ramaḍān with faith and for
reward in the world hereafter,
will be forgiven all his past sins.

ḤADĪTH OF AL-BUKHĀRĪ AND MUSLIM
ON THE AUTHORITY OF ABŪ HURAYRAH.

— 29 —

When Ramaḍān comes,
the doors of Heaven are opened,
the doors of Hell are closed,
the devils are put in chains,
and the doors of mercy are opened.

ḤADĪTH OF AL-BUKHĀRĪ. AND MUSLIM
ON THE AUTHORITY OF ABŪ HURAYRAH.

— 30 —

Anas ibn Mālik said that they used to
travel with the Prophet.
Those who observed a fast
never found fault with those who
did not keep the fast.
Similarly, those not observing the fast
never said anything amiss to those who
kept their fast.

ḤADĪTH OF AL-BUKHĀRĪ.

— 31 —

Any man who misses a fast without a
reason, such as illness,
can never atone for it,
even if he fasts for the rest of his life.

ḤADĪTH OF AT-TIRMIDHĪ AND
ABŪ DĀWŪD ON THE AUTHORITY OF ABŪ HURAYRAH.

— 32 —

Partake of *saḥūr* (food, taken a little before dawn during Ramaḍān), for there is a blessing in it.

ḤADĪTH OF AL-BUKHĀRĪ AND MUSLIM ON THE AUTHORITY OF ANAS IBN MĀLIK.

— 33 —

ʿAbdullāh ibn al-ʿAbbās reported that the Prophet made alms-giving on ʿĪd-ul-Fiṭr an obligatory act. As well as providing food for the poor, it was meant to atone for any absurdity or immodesty that may have been committed during fasting in the month of Ramaḍān.

ḤADĪTH OF ABŪ DĀWŪD.

— 34 —

When you pay *zakāt* (alms),
you have done your duty, as is obligatory.
But a person who amasses unlawful wealth and then makes gifts to the poor from it will have no spiritual reward for so doing.
On the contrary,
he will carry the burden of it with him into the next world.

ḤADĪTH OF IBN MĀJAH
ON THE AUTHORITY OF ABŪ HURAYRAH.

— 35 —

Allah has made the Muslims duty bound to pay *zakāt* (alms).
It will be realised from the wealthy to be distributed among the needy.

ḤADĪTH OF AL-BUKHĀRĪ AND MUSLIM
ON THE AUTHORITY OF ᶜABDULLĀH IBN AL-ᶜABBĀS.

— 36 —

The owner of any land which is irrigated by rain water or a stream, or which is situated close to a river, is obliged to give one tenth of its produce to the needy.
The owner of such land as is irrigated by other methods will pay half this amount.

ḤADĪTH OF AL-BUKHĀRĪ
ON THE AUTHORITY OF ᶜABDULLĀH IBN AL-ᶜABBĀS.

— 37 —

If a person to whom God has given
wealth does not give *zakāt* (alms),
he will find that,
on the Day of Judgement,
his wealth turns into a poisonous snake
with two black spots on its head.
It will be like a yoke around his neck.
Then it will seize him by the jaws and
declare,
'I am your wealth.
I am your treasure.'

ḤADĪTH OF AL-BUKHĀRĪ
ON THE AUTHORITY OF ABŪ HURAYRAH.

— 38 —

A believer, who feeds another of the
faithful who is hungry, will be fed on
the fruits of Paradise by God
on the Day of Judgement.
And a believer, who serves water
To another who is thirsty, will have
his thirst slaked from the sealed drinks
by God on the Day of Judgement.
And if a believer
clothes another of the faithful
who is in dire need of clothing,
he too will be rewarded with apparel
from Paradise by God on the
Day of Judgement.

ḤADĪTH OF AT-TIRMIDHĪ
ON THE AUTHORITY OF ABŪ SAᶜĪD AL-KHUDRĪ.

— 39 —

Abū Dharr al-Ghifārī relates that
he came to the Prophet, who was sitting
in the shade of the Kaʿbah. When he
saw me he said,
'They stand to lose.'
I said, 'May my parents ransom you. To
whom do you refer?'
'To those with an excess of riches,'
he replied, 'who just squander their
wealth, heedless of the fact that they can
be saved only if they spend generously
for a good cause. And there are very few
wealthy men of that ilk.'

ḤADĪTH OF AL-BUKHĀRĪ AND MUSLIM.

— 40 —

Giving alms to the poor
is a single good deed,
but giving alms to a poor relative has
the double virtue of giving alms and,
at the same time,
treating one's own relative well.

ḤADĪTH OF AN-NASĀ'Ī AND AT-TIRMIDHĪ
ON THE AUTHORITY OF SALMĀN IBN ʿĀMIR.

— 41 —

If a man who sets out with the
intention of performing Ḥajj,
ʿumrah or *jihād* meets with his death on
the way, he will be granted the rewards
of *jihād*, Ḥajj or *ʿumrah*
by his Maker.

ḤADĪTH OF AL-BAYHAQĪ
ON THE AUTHORITY OF ABŪ HURAYRAH.

— 42 —

Asked which deed inspired the greatest
respect, the Prophet replied,
'To believe in Allah and
His Messenger.'
When asked what ranked next in order
of merit, he said,
'To perform *jihād* for the sake
of Allah.'
Asked what came after that,
he replied *ḥajj mabrūr*, that is,
performing pilgrimage while remaining
free from sin.

ḤADĪTH OF AL-BUKHĀRĪ AND MUSLIM
ON THE AUTHORITY OF ABŪ HURAYRAH.

— 43 —

A man who decides to perform Hajj
should act with promptness,
for he may fall sick,
or his mount may get lost, or a need
may arise that becomes an obstacle.

ḤADĪTH OF IBN MĀJAH
ON THE AUTHORITY OF ʿABDULLĀH IBN AL-ʿABBĀS.

— 44 —

God's blessings are for everyone,
but a strong believer is better than a
weak one. Wish for things which are
beneficial to you, and in this,
seek God's help. Do not lose heart.
If you are visited by misfortune, do not
say, 'If I had done this or that, it could
have been averted.' Because 'if' opens
the door to Satan.

ḤADĪTH OF IBN MĀJAH
ON THE AUTHORITY OF ABŪ HURAYRAH.

— 45 —

Young man,
(the Prophet said to ʿAbdullāh ibn al-ʿAbbās) hear some words of advice:
Be mindful of God and God will protect you.
Be mindful of God and you will find Him before you.
If you ask, ask of God;
if you seek help, seek help of God.
Know that if all the people were to gather together to give you the benefit of anything, it would be something that God had already prescribed for you, and that if they gathered together to harm you with anything, this would only be as God had already ordained.

ḤADĪTH OF AT-TIRMIDHĪ.

— 46 —

Umm Salamah (the Prophet's wife)
recounts an incident which took place
when the Prophet was at home
with her. He called out
to the maid servant, and
when she failed to appear,
he showed signs of displeasure.
Then Umm Salamah peeped out
through the curtain and saw the maid
playing.
The Prophet, who was holding a *miswāk*
(a twig for cleaning the teeth) in his
hand, said to the maidservant,
'If I had had no fear
of retribution
on Judgement Day,
I would have hit you with this twig.'

AL-ADAB AL-MUFRAD BY IMĀM AL-BUKHĀRĪ.

— 47 —

On the Day of Judgement, from
amongst all those destined for Hell,
a particular man,
the richest man in the world,
will be brought forth and cast into Hell
for a moment.
Then he will be taken out
and will be asked, 'O son of Adam,
have you ever known the good things of life?
Have you ever seen comfortable days?'
And he will reply,
'By God, O Lord, never.'
Then from amongst all those
destined for Paradise,
one who has suffered the most in the world
will be brought forth
and will be allowed to enter Paradise
for a moment.
Then he will be taken out and asked,
'O son of Adam,

have you ever seen suffering?
Have you ever experienced hardship
in your life?'
He will reply, 'By God, no.
I have never suffered.
I have never undergone hardship.'*

ḤADĪTH OF MUSLIM
ON THE AUTHORITY OF ANAS IBN MĀLIK.

* THAT IS, JUST ONE MOMENT IN HELL
WOULD SUFFICE TO MAKE AN EVIL PERSON FORGET
ALL THE ENJOYMENT HE MAY HAVE HAD IN LIFE,
WHILE THE MERE SIGHT OF PARADISE
WOULD BE ENOUGH TO MAKE A RIGHTEOUS MAN
FORGET ALL THE SUFFERING
HE MAY HAVE EXPERIENCED IN THE LIFE
OF THIS WORLD.

— 48 —

According to Muʿādh ibn Jabal, when the Prophet appointed him governor of Yemen, he said, 'Abstain from luxuries, for those who live luxurious lives are no servants of God.'

ḤADĪTH OF AḤMAD IBN ḤANBAL.

— 49 —

A man who acquires a stretch of land
by tyranny
will be made to wear a yoke
made of seven earths around his neck
on the Day of Judgement.

ḤADĪTH OF AL-BUKHĀRĪ AND MUSLIM
ON THE AUTHORITY OF SAʿĪD IBN ZAYD.

— 50 —

A man may speak of God's pleasure
without giving it much importance
and yet be raised in status
by his Creator.
A man may say something which is
abhorrent to God,
without attaching any importance to it,
and it may sweep him
straight into Hell.

ḤADĪTH OF AL-BUKHĀRĪ
ON THE AUTHORITY OF ABŪ HURAYRAH.

— 51 —

'A man who has as much as an iota of arrogance in his heart will not enter Paradise.' Hearing these words of the Prophet, a man asked,
'What if a man likes to dress in good clothes and wear good shoes?'
The Prophet said, 'God himself possesses elegance. And He likes elegance. This has nothing to do with arrogance. A man is arrogant when he refuses to accept the truth and considers others to be inferior.'

ḤADĪTH OF MUSLIM
ON THE AUTHORITY OF ᶜABDULLĀH IBN MASᶜŪD.

— 52 —

God accepts the repentance of a man right to his last gasp, before he dies.

ḤADĪTH OF AT-TIRMIDHĪ
ON THE AUTHORITY OF ᶜABDULLĀH IBN ᶜUMAR.

— 53 —

Abū Dharr al-Ghifārī, who went to the Prophet for advice, was given this counsel:
'Fear God, for He is the one Who sets right all that concerns you. Read the Qur'ān and keep remembering God. For then you will be remembered in the heavens. And that will be a light for you on the earth.'

ḤADĪTH OF AḤMAD IBN ḤANBAL.

— 54 —

'The heart becomes rusted like iron in water.'
When asked how to banish this corrosion, the Prophet replied, 'Remember death frequently and recite the Qur'ān.'

ḤADĪTH OF AN-NASĀ'Ī
ON THE AUTHORITY OF ʿABDULLĀH IBN ʿUMAR.

— 55 —

According to Abū Hurayrah, the Prophet
recited a verse from the Qur'ān about
the Day the earth would give its account.
Then he asked,
'Do you know
what this account will be?'
His listeners replied,
'God and His Messenger know better.'
'The account
the earth will give,' said the Prophet,
'is the witness it will bear
to the deeds and misdeeds
all men and women have committed
throughout its length and breadth,
and to the exact moments of
their commission. That is what
the earth's account will be.'

ḤADĪTH OF AT-TIRMIDHĪ.

— 56 —

Following the rule of abstinence from worldly things does not mean that what is normally permitted becomes prohibited or that wealth should be allowed to go to waste. On the contrary, such abstinence means that you should place greater reliance on what God intends for you than on what you have in hand yourself. And when misfortune strikes, you should relish its continuance for the reward this will bring.

ḤADĪTH OF AT-TIRMIDHĪ
ON THE AUTHORITY OF ABŪ DHARR AL-GHIFĀRĪ.

— 57 —

Anyone who unjustly flogs his servant will be punished on the Day of Judgement.

ḤADĪTH OF AT-TABARĀNĪ
ON THE AUTHORITY OF ABŪ HURAYRAH.

— 58 —

Love for the life of this world is damaging to the life of the Hereafter. Anyone who values the life of the Hereafter will be indifferent to the life of this world. Therefore, prefer that which is eternal to that which is ephemeral.

ḤADĪTH OF AḤMAD IBN ḤANBAL
ON THE AUTHORITY OF ABŪ MŪSĀ AL-ASHʿARĪ.

— 59 —

Wise is he who controls his desires and prepares for the life which starts after death. And cast down is he who lives for the love of this world and has false expectations from God.

ḤADĪTH OF AT-TIRMIDHĪ
ON THE AUTHORITY OF SHADDĀD IBN AUS.

— 60 —

On the Day of Judgement the rightful will be given their due. So much so that a goat with horns will be avenged for the goat without horns.*

ḤADĪTH OF MUSLIM AND AT-TIRMIDHĪ
ON THE AUTHORITY OF ABŪ HURAYRAH.

* THAT IS, A PERSON WHO IS AS INSIGNIFICANT AS A GOAT WITHOUT HORNS WILL ALSO RECEIVE HIS DUE ON THAT DAY.

— 61 —

The lightest punishment for those in Hell will be two sparks under both feet. So searing will be their effect that the brain will begin to boil like a vessel on the fireplace.

ḤADĪTH OF AL-BUKHĀRĪ AND MUSLIM
ON THE AUTHORITY OF NUʿMĀN IBN BASHĪR.

— 62 —

On the Day of Judgement,
no step shall a man stir until he has answered questions on five aspects of his wordly existence:
his life and how he spent it;
his knowledge and what use he has made of it; his wealth, how he acquired it and how he has spent it;
and his body and how he has utilized it.

ḤADĪTH OF AT-TIRMIDHĪ
ON THE AUTHORITY OF ABŪ HURAYRAH.

— 63 —

The cautious man travels early in the morning. And the early morning traveller reaches his destination.
Pay heed. God's reward is peerless.
Pay heed. God's reward is Paradise.

ḤADĪTH OF AT-TIRMIDHĪ
ON THE AUTHORITY OF ABŪ HURAYRAH.

— 64 —

The man who enters Paradise will live in eternal blessedness. He will never be needy. Neither will his clothes wear out, nor will he lose his youth. Paradise has everything–things which have never been seen or heard of, and which are quite beyond human imagination.

ḤADĪTH OF MUSLIM
ON THE AUTHORITY OF ABŪ HURAYRAH.

— 65 —

According to Asmā' bint Abū Bakr, the Prophet once stood up and delivered a sermon in which he spoke of the trials that a man would be subjected to beyond the grave. When he delivered this discourse, the believers wept bitterly.

ḤADĪTH OF AL-BUKHĀRĪ.

— 66 —

When those destined for Paradise
enter it,
to each a herald will cry:
'Now you will enjoy good health
forever. You will never fall ill.
You will retain your youth forever.
You will never grow old.
You will be prosperous forever.
You will never be needy.
This is the essence of God's promise
to you.'
Then a cry will go up: 'This is
the Paradise you were promised.
You have been made its inheritor
in return for your
good deeds' (7:43).

ḤADĪTH OF MUSLIM AND AT-TIRMIDHĪ
ON THE AUTHORITY OF ABŪ HURAYRAH.

— 67 —

A man thus addressed the Prophet:
'O Messenger of God, who rightfully
deserves the best treatment from me?'
'Your mother,'
the Prophet said.
'Then who?'
the man asked again.
'Your mother,'
replied the Prophet.
'Then who?'
asked the man once again.
'Your mother,'
said the Prophet.
The man asked once more,
'Then who?'
'Your father,'
said the noble Prophet.

ḤADĪTH OF AL-BUKHĀRĪ AND MUSLIM
ON THE AUTHORITY OF ABŪ HURAYRAH.

— 68 —

The Prophet once exclaimed,
'Shame on him!
Shame on him!
Shame on him!'
When asked who the man in question
was, the Prophet replied,
'He is one who had both or one
of his parents with him in their old age,
yet he failed
to enter
Paradise.'

ḤADĪTH OF MUSLIM
ON THE AUTHORITY OF ABŪ HURAYRAH.

— 69 —

Abū Usayd as-Saʿīdī tells of how they
were once with the Prophet
when a man from the Banu Salmah
arrived in their midst.
Addressing the Prophet,
he asked, 'O Messenger of God,
Are there any outstanding debts
which I have to repay
after my parents' deaths?'
The Prophet, replied,
'Yes, pray for them
and seek forgiveness for them.
And fulfill their obligations now that
they are gone.
And treat their relations with kindness.
And respect
their friends.'

ḤADĪTH OF ABŪ DĀWŪD.

— 70 —

A man who treats his relatives well
in order to return their good treatment
of him shows no real love
for them.
The man who really shows love
for his relatives is one who
treats them well
despite their being unkind
to him.

ḤADĪTH OF AL-BUKHĀRĪ
ON THE AUTHORITY OF ʿABDULLĀH IBN ʿUMAR.

— 71 —

He who satiates himself,
while his immediate neighbours
go hungry,
is not a true believer.

ḤADĪTH OF AḤMAD IBN ḤANBAL
ON THE AUTHORITY OF ʿABDULLĀH IBN ʿABBĀS.

— 72 —

Asma' bint Abū Bakr related how her foster mother, a believer in polytheism *(shirk)*, had come to her during the period of the treaty of al-Hudaybiyyah. Concerned that her foster mother was a polytheist, she addressed the Prophet, 'O Messenger of God, my idolatrous *(mushrik)* mother has come to me and she wants something from me. Should I give it to her?' 'Yes. Treat her well,' replied the Prophet.

ḤADĪTH OF AL-BUKHĀRĪ AND MUSLIM.

— 73 —

A man who has two wives, but does not give them equal treatment, will find half his body lost on the Day of Judgement.

ḤADĪTH OF AT-TIRMIDHĪ
ON THE AUTHORITY OF ABŪ HURAYRAH.

— 74 —

When a man dies, nothing lives on after him, except for three things: *ṣadaqah jāriyah* (continuing charity),* knowledge which can benefit others, or virtuous offspring who will pray for him.

ḤADĪTH OF MUSLIM ON THE AUTHORITY OF ABŪ HURAYRAH.

* THAT IS, HIS CHARITY, THE BENEFIT OF WHICH CONTINUES EVEN AFTER THE DONOR HAS PASSED AWAY, SUCH AS THE BUILDING OF A BRIDGE OR A HOSPITAL, OR THE DIGGING OF A WELL.

— 75 —

A believer should never loathe a believing wife. If one quality in her does not find favour with her husband, some other quality will be to his liking.

ḤADĪTH OF MUSLIM ON THE AUTHORITY OF ABŪ HURAYRAH.

— 76 —

A man once went to the Prophet with a grievance against his relatives. 'O Messenger of God,' he said, 'I have some relatives whom I treat with kindness. Yet they show me no kindness. I treat them well and they treat me badly. I show them forbearance and they treat me with brutality.' The Prophet replied, 'If you are as you say you are, then it is as if you have smeared their faces with dust. And you will always have God's help against them so long as you continue to be well-behaved towards them.'

ḤADĪTH OF MUSLIM
ON THE AUTHORITY OF ABŪ HURAYRAH.

— 77 —

When the Prophet Muḥammad ﷺ was asked who was the best of all women, he replied, 'The woman whose husband feels pleased to see her, who obeys when her husband commands, and who does not take a stand about her or her wealth which is displeasing to her husband.'

ḤADĪTH OF AN-NASĀ'Ī
ON THE AUTHORITY OF ABŪ HURAYRAH.

— 78 —

When a man spends on his family members with the intention of seeking God's pleasure, then his spending becomes an act of charity.

ḤADĪTH OF AL-BUKHĀRĪ AND MUSLIM
ON THE AUTHORITY OF ABŪ MASʿŪD.

— 79 —

A person once said to the Prophet,
'O Messenger of God, a certain woman
is said to offer *ṣalāt* (prayers), observe
fasts and give alms generously,
but she hurts her neighbours
by the way she speaks.'
The Prophet replied,
'She will go to Hell.'
Then the man said,
'O Messenger of God, a certain other
woman says fewer prayers, keeps fewer
fasts voluntarily and offers little in the
way of alms. She only gives a few pieces
of cheese.
But she never hurts her neighbours
with her tongue.'
The Prophet replied,
'She will enter Paradise.'

ḤADĪTH OF AḤMAD IBN ḤANBAL
ON THE AUTHORITY OF ABŪ HURAYRAH.

— 80 —

When the Prophet was asked by
ʿĀ'ishah to which of two neighbours she
should send a gift, he replied,
'To the one whose door is closer to your
own.'

ḤADĪTH OF AL-BUKHĀRĪ.

— 81 —

The Prophet once exclaimed,
'By God, he is not a believer!
By God, he is not a believer!
By God, he is not a believer!'
The people asked,
'O Messenger of God, who?'
'The man whose excesses prevent his
neighbour from living in peace,'
replied the noble Prophet.

ḤADĪTH OF AL-BUKHĀRĪ
ON THE AUTHORITY OF ABŪ HURAYRAH.

— 82 —

A believer is a mirror to another believer.
A believer is a brother to another believer.
He saves him from losses.
He safeguards his interests in his absence.

ḤADĪTH OF ABŪ DĀWŪD
ON THE AUTHORITY OF ABŪ HURAYRAH.

— 83 —

According to Anas ibn Mālik, the Prophet said to him, 'O my son, if you can act in such a way that you spend your mornings and your evenings without wishing anyone ill, then that is how you should always act.' Then he added, 'O my son, this is my way. And anyone who loves my ways, loves me. And anyone who loves me will live with me in Paradise.'

ḤADĪTH OF MUSLIM.

— 84 —

Each one of you is a shepherd.
And each one of you will be asked about your flock.
A ruler also is a shepherd and he will be asked about his flock.
And every man is a shepherd to his family.
And a woman is the custodian of her husband's house and his children.
Thus each one of you is a shepherd, and each one will be asked about his flock.

ḤADĪTH OF AL-BUKHĀRĪ AND MUSLIM
ON THE AUTHORITY OF ʿABDULLĀH IBN ʿUMAR.

— 85 —

You should visit the sick, feed the hungry and set prisoners free.

ḤADĪTH OF AL-BUKHĀRĪ
ON THE AUTHORITY OF ABŪ MŪSĀ AL-ASHʿARĪ.

— 86 —

Whenever God makes a man responsible for other people, whether in greater or lesser numbers, he will be questioned as to whether he ruled his charges in accordance with God's decrees or not. And that will not be all. God will question him even about his family members.

ḤADĪTH OF AḤMAD IBN ḤANBAL
ON THE AUTHORITY OF ʿABDULLĀH IBN ʿUMAR.

— 87 —

If you show kindness to your servant while employing him in some task, this will weigh heavily in your favour on the Day of Judgement. That will be your reward.

ḤADĪTH OF ʿAMR IBN HURAYTH.

— 88 —

The best person among you is the one
who treats his family members well. And
I am the best person
for my family.

ḤADĪTH OF IBN MĀJAH
ON THE AUTHORITY OF ᶜABDULLĀH IBN AL-ᶜABBĀS.

— 89 —

When the Prophet was asked which
form of Islam was better, he replied,
'To feed the people and extend greetings
of peace
to them–
be they of your acquaintance
or not.'

ḤADĪTH OF AL-BUKHĀRĪ AND MUSLIM
ON THE AUTHORITY OF ᶜABDULLĀH IBN ᶜAMR IBN AL-ᶜĀṢ.

— 90 —

On the Day of Judgement, God will say,
'O son of Adam, I was sick, but you
did not visit Me.'
The man will reply,
'O my Lord, how could I visit You– the
Lord of the whole universe?'
God will say, 'Did you not know that
such and such a man had fallen ill?
Yet you did not visit him.
Did you not know that had you gone
there to visit him, you would have found
Me there with him?'

ḤADĪTH OF MUSLIM
ON THE AUTHORITY OF ABŪ HURAYRAH.

— 91 —

O Muslim women, do not belittle the gift of any woman in your neighbourhood, even if it happens to be a goat's hoof.

ḤADĪTH OF AL-BUKHĀRĪ AND MUSLIM ON THE AUTHORITY OF ABŪ HURAYRAH.

— 92 —

According to Anas ibn Mālik, when God's Messenger said, 'Help your brother, irrespective of whether he is the oppressor or the oppressed,' a man said, 'O Messenger of God, I can help the oppressed, but how can I help the oppressor?' The Prophet replied, 'Stop him from committing an act of oppression. That in itself is a form of help.'

ḤADĪTH OF AL-BUKHĀRĪ AND MUSLIM.

— 93 —

According to ʿAbdullāh ibn ʿUmar, the Prophet, addressing the people on the occasion of the farewell pilgrimage, exhorted them to listen carefully to what he had to say:

'All Muslims are brothers.
They constitute one brotherhood.
Nothing belonging to one Muslim
can become legitimate property
of another, unless it has been freely and willingly given. Do not, therefore, do injustice to your own selves. O God,
have I conveyed your message?
Woe betide you. When I am gone,
do not become infidels
and start killing each other.'

ḤADĪTH OF AL-BUKHĀRĪ.

— 94 —

Do not marry women for their beauty. It is possible that their beauty may destroy them. Do not marry them for their wealth. It is possible that their wealth may make them rebellious. Instead, marry them on the basis of their faith. And a black maid who is a believer is much better for you.

ḤADĪTH OF IBN MĀJAH
ON THE AUTHORITY OF ᶜABDULLĀH IBN ᶜAMR IBN AL-ᶜĀṢ.

— 95 —

The worst feast is the marriage feast to which the rich are invited and the poor are not. And anyone who does not accept an invitation commits an act of disobedience against God and His Messenger.

ḤADĪTH OF AL-BUKHĀRĪ AND MUSLIM
ON THE AUTHORITY OF ABŪ HURAYRAH.

— 96 —

According to Jarīr ibn ʿAbdullāh, when he asked the Prophet about a man's gaze falling inadvertently on a strange woman, the Prophet replied,
'Turn your eyes away.'

ḤADĪTH OF MUSLIM.

— 97 —

O young people, those among you who are able
must enter into marriage. For
it helps to divert your attention from women. And
it is a safeguard
against lust.
And those who cannot marry should observe fasts, for fasting too
is a safeguard.

ḤADĪTH OF AL-BUKHĀRĪ AND MUSLIM
ON THE AUTHORITY OF ʿABDULLĀH IBN MASʿŪD.

— 98 —

There are four reasons for a man to
marry a woman:
her wealth;
her lineage;
her beauty;
her faith.
Woe betide you!
Only enter into marriage with one who
has faith.

ḤADĪTH OF AL-BUKHĀRĪ AND MUSLIM
ON THE AUTHORITY OF ABŪ HURAYRAH.

— 99 —

The best gift from a father to his child
is education and upbringing.

ḤADĪTH OF AT-TIRMIDHĪ
ON THE AUTHORITY OF SAʿĪD IBN AL-ʿĀṢ.

— 100 —

The best dower is the easy one.

ḤADĪTH OF ABŪ DĀWŪD
ON THE AUTHORITY OF ŪQBAH IBN ʿĀMĪR.

— 101 —

Should I not tell you what is the best charity? To spend on the daughter who has been returned to you (a divorced or widowed daughter), when there is no one else to earn for her.

ḤADĪTH OF IBN MĀJAH
ON THE AUTHORITY OF SURAQA IBN MĀLIK.

— 102 —

According to ʿĀ'ishah, once when a child was brought to the Prophet, he fondled him and said, 'These children make cowards and misers of the parents. And they are the flowers of the Almighty.'

ḤADĪTH OF IBN MĀJAH.

— 103 —

According to ʿAbdullāh ibn al-ʿAbbās, the Prophet cursed those men who try to resemble women
and women who try
to resemble men.

ḤADĪTH OF AL-BUKHĀRĪ ABŪ DĀWŪD AND AN-NASĀ'Ī.

— 104 —

On the Day of Judgement, what will weigh most heavily in favour of the believer will be his good morals. God abhors those who indulge in shameless talk and use indecent language.

ḤADĪTH OF AT-TIRMIDHĪ
ON THE AUTHORITY OF ABŪ'D DARDĀ.

— 105 —

Save yourselves from envy.
For envy eats up virtue
as fire eats up wood.

ḤADĪTH OF ABŪ DĀWŪD
ON THE AUTHORITY OF ABŪ HURAYRAH.

— 106 —

It is not proper
for a man to keep away
from his brother for more than
three days, and then when they meet to
turn their faces away from
each other.
The better of the two is the one who
greets the other first.

ḤADĪTH OF AL-BUKHĀRĪ AND MUSLIM
ON THE AUTHORITY OF ABŪ AYYŪB AL-ANṢĀRĪ.

— 107 —

An honest and trustworthy merchant (in the world hereafter) will be with the Prophets, the truthful and the martyrs.

ḤADĪTH OF AT-TIRMIDHĪ
ON THE AUTHORITY OF ABŪ SAᶜĪD AL-KHUDRĪ.

— 108 —

According to Abū Mūsā al-Ashᶜarī,
the Prophet said,
'Believers are like the
different parts of a building, each one
supporting the other.'
Then he demonstrated what he meant
by interlocking his fingers.

ḤADĪTH OF AL-BUKHĀRĪ AND MUSLIM.

— 109 —

How evil is the man who hoards essential supplies! If God wills it that the prices of merchandise fall, that makes him unhappy.
But if the prices rise, that makes him happy.

ḤADĪTH OF AL-BAYHAQĪ ON THE AUTHORITY OF MUʿĀDH.

— 110 —

You will observe that the believers are like the parts of the body in relation to each other in matters of kindness, love and affection. When one part of the body is afflicted, the entire body feels it; there is loss of sleep and a fever develops.

ḤADĪTH OF AL-BUKHĀRĪ AND MUSLIM
ON THE AUTHORITY OF NUʿMĀN IBN BASHĪR.

— 111 —

To earn through labour is the best way
to earn, provided the work
is done
with sincerity.

ḤADĪTH OF AḤMAD IBN ḤANBAL
ON THE AUTHORITY OF ABŪ HURAYRAH.

— 112 —

It is obligatory for a Muslim to pay heed to his ruler and obey him, whether he likes him or not, as long as the ruler does not order him to commit a sin. If he orders him to sin, then he is not to pay heed to him or obey him.

ḤADĪTH OF AL-BUKHĀRĪ AND MUSLIM
ON THE AUTHORITY OF ʿABDULLĀH IBN ʿUMAR.

— 113 —

Muslims are brothers. When one Muslim sells something to another, it is his duty to inform the other of any defect in the merchandise.

ḤADĪTH OF IBN MĀJAH
ON THE AUTHORITY OF ʿUQBAH IBN ʿĀMIR.

— 114 —

Avoid falling under suspicion.
For suspicion does the worst damage.
Do not inquire into the lives of others.
Do not pry.
Do not exaggerate what others say.
Bear each other no malice, and
do not hurt each others' interests.
And, by being brothers to each other
become the servants of God.

ḤADĪTH OF MUSLIM
ON THE AUTHORITY OF ABŪ HURAYRAH.

— 115 —

The best sustenance is that which you earn by your own industry. The Prophet Dāwūd (David) عليه السلام used to earn his sustenance with his own hands.

ḤADĪTH OF AL-BUKHĀRĪ
ON THE AUTHORITY OF MIQDAM IBN MAʿDĪKARIB.

— 116 —

According to Suhayl when God's Messenger passed by a camel and noticed that it had become so thin that its back and its stomach seemed to be touching, he said, 'Fear God when dealing with these beasts. Mount them when they are in good condition, and leave them in that same state.'

ḤADĪTH OF ABŪ DĀWŪD.

— 117 —

A merchant who hoards goods in order to raise their price is a sinner.

ḤADĪTH OF MUSLIM ON THE AUTHORITY OF MAʿMAR.

— 118 —

According to Rāfiʿ ibn Khadīj, when the Prophet was asked which was the best kind of earning, he replied, 'That for which a man works with his hands. And honest trading.'

ḤADĪTH OF AḤMAD IBN ḤANBAL.

— 119 —

A time will come when people will no longer care about whether their wealth has been lawfully or unlawfully acquired.

ḤADĪTH OF AL-BUKHĀRĪ
ON THE AUTHORITY OF ABŪ HURAYRAH.

— 120 —

It is not just
for a man to sell his merchandise
without disclosing its defects.
It is proper for the vendor to
tell the buyer of any defects
of which he is aware.

ḤADĪTH OF AḤMAD IBN ḤANBAL
ON THE AUTHORITY OF WATHILAH.

— 121 —

The trader who does not hoard essential
supplies receives
His sustenance,
while the hoarder of essential supplies
is cursed.

ḤADĪTH OF IBN MĀJAH AND AD-DĀRIMĪ
ON THE AUTHORITY OF ʿUMAR IBN AL-KHAṬṬAB.

— 122 —

Allah will show compassion to those who show kindness while buying and selling, and recovering debts.

ḤADĪTH OF AL-BUKHĀRĪ ON THE AUTHORITY OF JĀBIR.

— 123 —

One who denies an heir his legacy will be denied the legacy of Paradise by the Almighty.

ḤADĪTH OF IBN MĀJAH
ON THE AUTHORITY OF ANAS IBN MĀLIK.

— 124 —

One who makes sacrifices for the sake of God will have all his sins pardoned, except for his debts.

ḤADĪTH OF MUSLIM
ON THE AUTHORITY OF ʿABDULLĀH IBN ʿUMAR.

— 125 —

Pay the labourer his wages even before
his sweat dries up.

ḤADĪTH OF IBN MĀJAH
ON THE AUTHORITY OF ʿABDULLĀH IBN ʿUMAR.

— 126 —

There was a man who used to give
loans to poor people. When his assistant
had to go to them to recover the loans,
he would urge him to be forgiving to
those who were not able to pay back his
loans with ease, believing that, in that
way,
perhaps God would show him
forgiveness.
When that man came face to face with
the Almighty, He forgave him.

ḤADĪTH OF AL-BUKHĀRĪ AND MUSLIM
ON THE AUTHORITY OF ABŪ HURAYRAH.

— 127 —

If a man commits something to your care, be sure to return it to him. Never betray anyone's trust, not even if the person concerned has failed to stand by his commitments to you.

ḤADĪTH OF AT-TIRMIDHĪ
ON THE AUTHORITY OF ABŪ HURAYRAH.

— 128 —

Save yourself from the curse of an oppressed person, who seeks his rights from God, for God never denies the righteous their rights.

ḤADĪTH OF AL-BAYHAQĪ
ON THE AUTHORITY OF ʿALI IBN ABĪ ṬĀLIB.

— 129 —

If a Muslim farms the land or plants a tree, and then a bird, a beast or a man eats something from it, he receives in return the reward of a charity.

ḤADĪTH OF MUSLIM
ON THE AUTHORITY OF ANAS IBN MĀLIK.

— 130 —

What is lawful and what is forbidden are both quite clear. But between them are matters which are not clear. A man who avoids the unclear will be even more careful to avoid an open sin. But it is feared that a man who does not baulk at unclear sins will indulge even in open sin. And sin is like a grazing ground forbidden by God. A beast that passes by it risks the chance of straying into it.

ḤADĪTH OF AL-BUKHĀRĪ AND MUSLIM
ON THE AUTHORITY OF NUᶜMĀN IBN BASHĪR.

— 131 —

On the Day of Judgement, God will not even look at a man who, in a show of arrogance, lets his clothes sweep the ground. Abū Bakr said, 'The cloth which I have worn around my waist trails no matter what I do.' To this the Prophet said, 'You are not one of those who do it out of arrogance.'

ḤADĪTH OF AL-BUKHĀRĪ
ON THE AUTHORITY OF ᶜABDULLĀH IBN ᶜUMAR.

— 132 —

One who walks with a tyrant,
in the full knowledge that he is a tyrant,
in order to strengthen him,
is such as has already left the fold
of Islam.

ḤADĪTH OF AL-BAYHAQĪ
ON THE AUTHORITY OF AUS IBN SHURAḤABĪL.

— 133 —

A man who borrows things, with the intention of returning them, has them returned on his behalf by the Almighty.
A man who borrows things, with no intention of returning them, has such possessions destroyed by the Almighty.

ḤADĪTH OF AL-BUKHĀRĪ
ON THE AUTHORITY OF ABŪ HURAYRAH.

— 134 —

Anger is the devil,
and the devil has been created from fire.
And fire is extinguished by water,
therefore, when any of you feel angry,
you should perform your ablutions.

ḤADĪTH OF ABŪ DĀWŪD
ON THE AUTHORITY OF ʿATIYAH SAʿDĪ.

— 135 —

When any of you feel angry, you should sit down if you are standing. And if your anger passes off with this, well and good. If not, you should lie down.

ḤADĪTH OF ABŪ DĀWŪD
ON THE AUTHORITY OF ABŪ DHARR AL-GHIFĀRĪ.

— 136 —

When a man tells you something in confidence, you must not betray his trust.

ḤADĪTH OF ABŪ DĀWŪD
ON THE AUTHORITY OF JĀBIR IBN ʿABDULLĀH.

— 137 —

On the Day of Judgement, the tyrant's own tyranny will descend upon him in the form of darkness.

ḤADĪTH OF AL-BUKHĀRĪ AND MUSLIM
ON THE AUTHORITY OF ʿABDULLĀH IBN ʿUMAR.

— 138 —

When there are three of you, one should not be left out while the other two share a secret, for this will cause him grief.

ḤADĪTH OF AḤMAD IBN ḤANBAL
ON THE AUTHORITY OF ᶜABDULLĀH IBN ᶜUMAR.

— 139 —

Whosoever of you sees an evil action, let him change it with his hand;
and if he is not able to do so,
then with his tongue;
and if he is not able to do so,
then with his heart, for that is the minimum that is desirable from a believer.

ḤADĪTH OF AN-NASĀ'Ī
ON THE AUTHORITY OF ABŪ SAᶜĪD AL-KHUDRĪ.

— 140 —

No one should have to ask another to vacate his seat for him. Room should be made for him without his asking.

ḤADĪTH OF AḤMAD
ON THE AUTHORITY OF ʿABDULLĀH IBN ʿUMAR.

— 141 —

It is not proper for a man to sit between two men and thus separate them, without seeking their permission.

ḤADĪTH OF ABŪ DĀWŪD AND
AT-TIRMIDHĪ ON THE AUTHORITY OF ʿAMR IBN SHUʿAYB.

— 142 —

Those who take bribes and those who give bribes are cursed by God.

ḤADĪTH OF AL-BUKHĀRĪ AND MUSLIM
ON THE AUTHORITY OF ʿABDULLĀH IBN ʿAMR IBN AL-ʿĀṢ.

— 143 —

By his own account, ʿAmr ibn ʿAbasah
met the Prophet in Mecca in the early
days of his prophethood, and asked him,
'What are you?'
He replied, 'I am a Prophet.'
ʿAmr then asked,
'What is a Prophet?'
He replied, 'I have been sent by God.'
'What has God sent you with?'
ʿAmr asked.
'With the commandment to destroy idols
and to treat one's relatives with
kindness;
to believe in one God and not to treat
anyone as His partner,' replied the
Prophet.

ḤADĪTH OF MUSLIM.

— 144 —

Three things are part of the good morals
of a believer.
When he is overcome by anger,
his anger should not drive him to
falsehood.
When he is happy,
his happiness should not take him
beyond the bounds of what is right.
When he has power,
he should not stake a claim to
something which is not his.

ḤADĪTH OF AṬ-ṬABARĀNĪ
ON THE AUTHORITY OF ANAS IBN MĀLIK.

— 145 —

The way to atone for slander is to pray for the forgiveness of the person whom you have slandered. Say, 'O God, forgive me as well as him.'

ḤADĪTH OF AL-JAMIᶜ AṢ-ṢAGHĪR
ON THE AUTHORITY OF ANAS IBN MĀLIK.

— 146 —

Explaining verse 41:34 of the Qur'ān,
ʿAbdullāh ibn ʿAbbās said that those
who exercised self-restraint when angry,
or when confronted by mischief,
would be protected
by God.
He would force their enemies
to bow down before them as if
they were His dear friends.

ḤADĪTH OF AL-BUKHĀRĪ.

— 147 —

Whenever a believer is striken with any hardship, or pain, or anxiety, or sorrow, or harm, or distress—even if it be a thorn that has hurt him—Allah redeems thereby some of his failings.

ḤADĪTH OF AL-BUKHĀRĪ AND MUSLIM.

— 148 —

Anas ibn Mālik relates that as he was walking with the Prophet, who happened to have a thick-bordered Najrānī *burd* (sheet) around his shoulders, a Bedouin came up to him and tugged at it.
'I saw that it had left a mark on his neck. Then the Bedouin said,
"O Muḥammad, order some of the wealth of God which you have in your possession to be given to me."
The Prophet looked at him and smiled, then he gave orders for something to be given to him.'

ḤADĪTH OF AL-BUKHĀRĪ AND MUSLIM.

— 149 —

A bedouin once urinated in the Prophet's Mosque, and people got up to punish him. The Prophet said, 'Leave him alone, and throw a bucket of water over his urine.

You are here to make things easy, not to make things difficult.'

ḤADĪTH OF AL-BUKHĀRĪ
ON THE AUTHORITY OF ABŪ HURAYRAH.

— 150 —

According to ʿĀ'ishah, the Prophet used to cobble his shoes, stitch his clothes and do the kind of housework that is done in all homes. He was a human being just like anybody else. He used to milk his goat and do sundry other chores himself.

ḤADĪTH OF AT-TIRMIDHĪ.

— 151 —

According to ʿĀ'ishah, the Prophet never gave others tasks which were beyond their capabilities.

ḤADĪTH OF AL-BUKHĀRĪ.

— 152 —

According to ʿAbdullāh ibn ʿAmr ibn al-ʿĀṣ, the Prophet was never seen to eat while reclining on a pillow. And no one had seen even two men walking behind him at any time.

ḤADĪTH OF ABŪ DĀWŪD.

— 153 —

ʿĀ'ishah said that she had never seen the Prophet show off his palate. He used just to smile.

ḤADĪTH OF AL-BUKHĀRĪ AND MUSLIM.

— 154 —

Sā'ib has thus recorded his commendation of the Prophet; 'In the period of Ignorance (i.e. before Islam) when you were my partner in business, you were the finest of all partners. You never deceived me. Neither did you quarrel with me.'

ḤADĪTH OF ABŪ DĀWŪD.

— 155 —

According to Yaʿala when he asked Umm Salamah how the Prophet recited the Qur'ān, she replied, 'The Prophet used to recite the Qur'ān with great clarity. Each word could be heard distinctly.'

ḤADĪTH OF AT-TIRMIDHĪ.

— 156 —

According to Jābir, the Prophet never said 'no' to any request.

ḤADĪTH OF AL-BUKHĀRĪ AND MUSLIM.

— 157 —

ʿAbdullāh ibn Masʿūd told how during the battle of Badr, one camel was shared by three men, namely Abū Lubabah, ʿAlī ibn Abī Ṭālib, and the Prophet. When it was the Prophet's turn to walk, the other two would say to him, 'Mount the camel. We will walk in your place.' The Prophet would reply, 'Neither of you is stronger than I am, nor am I less eager for rewards than you.'

ḤADĪTH OF AḤMAD IBN ḤANBAL.

— 158 —

Abū Hurayrah relates how the Prophet never criticised food.
'If he liked it, he ate it. If he did not, he just left it.'

ḤADĪTH OF AL-BUKHĀRĪ AND MUSLIM.

— 159 —

According to ʿAbdullāh ibn Masʿūd, the Prophet said that none of his Companions should complain to him of another. 'I would like to come to you with a clear heart.'

ḤADĪTH OF ABŪ DĀWŪD.

— 160 —

According to ʿĀ'ishah, the Prophet held that cleaning the teeth helped in maintaining oral hygiene. 'And,' said the Prophet, 'it gives pleasure to the Lord.'

ḤADĪTH OF AḤMAD IBN ḤANBAL AND AN-NASĀ'Ī.

— 161 —

Verily, God Almighty, and His angels,
and those who inhabit the heavens,
even the ants in their holes and
the fishes in their waters,
bless the good teachers of mankind.

ḤADĪTH OF AT-TIRMIDHĪ
ON THE AUTHORITY OF ABŪ UMĀMAH.

— 162 —

You will not enter Paradise
unless you have faith,
and you cannot be one of the faithful
unless you love each other.
Should I not tell you things which,
if followed,
will create love among you?
One is to observe the practice of greeting
each other.

ḤADĪTH OF MUSLIM
ON THE AUTHORITY OF ABŪ HURAYRAH.

— 163 —

According to ʿAbdullāh ibn al-ʿAbbās, the Prophet forbade the staging of fights between animals.

ḤADĪTH OF AT-TIRMIDHĪ.

— 164 —

According to ʿAbdullāh ibn ʿUmar, the Prophet forbade not only indulgence in slander and backbiting, but even listening to such talk.

MISHKĀT AL-MAṢĀBĪḤ.

— 165 —

When a man makes a promise with the intention of fulfilling it, but for some valid reason is unable to do so, he does not thereby commit a sin.

ḤADĪTH OF ABŪ DĀWŪD
ON THE AUTHORITY OF ZAYD IBN ARQAM.

— 166 —

According to Khuraym ibn Fatik, the Prophet rose after the completion of his morning prayer and said, 'The giving of false evidence is like committing idolatry.' He repeated this three times. Then he recited this passage of the Qur'ān: 'Shun the loathsome evil of idolatrous beliefs and practices; and shun every word that is untrue. Dedicate yourselves to God and serve none besides Him' (22:30-31).

ḤADĪTH OF ABŪ DĀWŪD.

— 167 —

'The man who indulges in backbiting will not enter Paradise!'

ḤADĪTH OF BUKHĀRĪ
ON THE AUTHORITY OF ABŪ HURAYRAH.

— 168 —

A man once asked the Prophet if bigotry
was to love one's tribe.
'No,' replied the Prophet.
'Bigotry is to help your tribe to tyrannise
others.'

ḤADĪTH OF IBN MĀJAH ON THE
AUTHORITY OF ʿUBADAH IBN KATHĪR ASH-SHĀMĪ.

— 169 —

He who preaches bigotry
is not one of us.
And not being one of us,
he may go ahead
and fight in the cause of bigotry.
He who dies for such a cause
is not one of us either.

ḤADĪTH OF ABŪ DĀWŪD
ON THE AUTHORITY OF JUBAYR IBN MUṬʿIM.

— 170 —

According to Abū Hurayrah, the Prophet once asked his listners if they knew what slander was, to which they replied that God and His Messenger knew better. The Prophet then explained that slander meant speaking of one's brother in a manner that was hurtful to him.

He was then asked, what if one's brother was actually at fault. The Prophet replied that, if he was at fault, then what was said against him was just backbiting and, if he was not, it was calumny.

ḤADĪTH OF MUSLIM
ON THE AUTHORITY OF ABŪ HURAYRAH.

— 171 —

'On the Day of Judgement, you will discover the worst man to be the one who had two faces.'

ḤADĪTH OF AL-BUKHĀRĪ AND MUSLIM ON THE AUTHORITY OF ABŪ HURAYRAH.

— 172 —

ʿAbdullāh said that it was not proper to tell lies
either in serious or in light vein.
Neither was it proper to make promises to one's children and then not fulfill them.

AL-ADAB AL-MUFRAD BY IMĀM AL-BUKHĀRĪ

— 173 —

There are four characteristics which together make a person a complete hypocrite.
The taint of hypocrisy will attach to the trustee who breaks his trust, to the speaker who tells untruths, to the maker of promises who fails to keep them and to the man who uses foul language when in disagreement with others.
This taint will remain unless the wrongdoer mends his ways.

ḤADĪTH OF AL-BUKHĀRĪ AND MUSLIM
ON THE AUTHORITY OF ʿABDULLĀH IBN ʿAMR IBN AL-ʿĀS.

— 174 —

When three men travel together, they should make one of them their leader.

ḤADĪTH OF ABŪ DĀWŪD
ON THE AUTHORITY OF ABŪ SAʿĪD AL-KHUDRI.

— 175 —

Do not quarrel with your brother.
Do not ridicule him.
You should refrain from making
a promise
and then going back on it.

ḤADĪTH OF AT-TIRMIDHĪ
ON THE AUTHORITY OF ABDULLĀH IBN AL-ʿABBĀS.

— 176 —

A man who helps his people
for an unjust cause
can be compared with a man,
who catches hold of the tail of a camel
which is falling into a well.

ḤADĪTH OF ABŪ DĀWŪD
ON THE AUTHORITY OF ʿABDULLĀH IBN MASʿŪD.

— 177 —

It is ruinous for a man to tell lies so
that others may laugh.
It is ruinous for him.
It is ruinous for him.

ḤADĪTH OF AT-TIRMIDHĪ
ON THE AUTHORITY OF BAHZ IBN ḤAKĪM.

— 178 —

Do not rejoice in the misfortunes of
your brother.
For God may show him compassion,
but create difficulties for you.

ḤADĪTH OF AT-TIRMIDHĪ
ON THE AUTHORITY OF WATHILAH.

— 179 —

The most perfect of believers, in point
of faith, is he who is the best in manners.

ḤADĪTH OF ABŪ DĀWŪD
ON THE AUTHORITY OF ABŪ HURAYRAH.

— 180 —

Even if a group of people in a jungle number only three, it is still incumbent upon them to choose a leader.

ḤADĪTH OF ABŪ DĀWŪD
ON THE AUTHORITY OF ᶜABDULLĀH IBN ᶜAMR.

— 181 —

None of you (truly) believes, until he wishes for his brother what he wishes for himself.

ḤADĪTH OF BUKHĀRĪ
ON THE AUTHORITY OF ANAS IBN MĀLIK.

— 182 —

Calling God in personal prayer is worship.

ḤADĪTH OF ABŪ DĀWŪD AND AT-TIRMIDHĪ
ON THE AUTHORITY OF NUᶜMĀN IBN BASHĪR.

— 183 —

O God,
only You can change our hearts.
We beseech You to do so,
so that we may submit to You.

ḤADĪTH OF MUSLIM ON THE AUTHORITY OF ᶜABDULLĀH IBN ᶜAMR IBN AL-ᶜĀṢ.

— 184 —

According to Abū Bakr aṣ-Ṣiddīq, when he asked the Prophet to tell him of some invocations which he could recite in his prayers, the Prophet said, 'Say, God, I have been an oppressor to myself. And there is no one but You who can forgive my sins. Therefore forgive me in Your generosity. And show me compassion. Verily, You are Forgiving and Compassionate.'

ḤADĪTH OF AT-TIRMIDHĪ AND MUSLIM.

— 185 —

According to Muʿādh, the Prophet took
his hand in his own and said,
'O Muʿādh, by God, I love You.' Then
he said, 'I give you this counsel: after
each prayer,
you must not omit to say,
"O God, help me to remember You,
and thank You, and worship You with
devotion."'

ḤADĪTH OF ABŪ DĀWŪD AND AN-NASĀ'Ī.

— 186 —

Ṭāriq ibn Ahyam relates that when
anyone entered the fold of Islam, the
Prophet would teach him to pray. Then
he would instruct him how to invoke
his Maker in these words:
'O God, forgive me and have mercy
on me. Give me prosperity and sustenance.'

ḤADĪTH OF MUSLIM.

— 187 —

God has given utterance to these words: 'We are with Our servant whenever he remembers Us; when his lips are busy for Us.'

ḤADĪTH OF BUKHĀRĪ
ON THE AUTHORITY OF ABŪ HURAYRAH.

— 188 —

O God, I have obtained one promise from You. And on no account will You go against it. After all, I am a human being. (If ever) I have harmed a Muslim, or have spoken ill of him, or cursed him, or flogged him, then in compensation for all this, give him Your blessings, Your purity and Your nearness.

ḤADĪTH OF AL-BUKHĀRĪ AND MUSLIM
ON THE AUTHORITY OF ABŪ HURAYRAH.

— 189 —

O God, I seek Your protection from misery and grief,
from weakness and laziness,
and from the burden of loans
and from things that will make others overcome me.

ḤADĪTH OF AL-BUKHĀRĪ AND MUSLIM ON THE AUTHORITY OF ANAS IBN MĀLIK.

— 190 —

ʿĀ'ishah related how she heard the Prophet praying thus: 'O God, be lenient with me while judging me.' When she asked him what leniency of judgement meant, he said, 'God's forgiveness after He has seen a man's record. O ʿĀ'ishah, anyone who is judged strictly will be ruined.'

ḤADĪTH OF AḤMAD IBN ḤANBAL.

— 191 —

According to Abū Saʿīd al-Khudrī, the
Prophet said, 'Whenever one of the
faithful invokes blessings which involve
no sin or the breaking up of a
relationship, God is certain to grant
one of three things.
Either He gives the supplicant His
blessings
in this world,
or He keeps them for him in the world
hereafter, or
He saves him from some misfortune.'
His listener then said,
'Now we shall invoke God's blessings
even more.'
'God's blessings are boundless,'
replied the Prophet.

ḤADĪTH OF AḤMAD IBN ḤANBAL.

— 192 —

This is the invocation of
a troubled man:
'O Allah I am a petitioner for Divine Mercy. Do not abandon me even for a moment to any desires. And keep all my affairs in order. There is no God but You.'

ḤADĪTH OF ABŪ DĀWŪD
ON THE AUTHORITY OF ABŪ BAKR.

— 193 —

God is nearest to His servant in the last phase of the night.
If possible,
be one of those
who remember God during this period.

ḤADĪTH OF AT-TIRMIDHĪ
ON THE AUTHORITY OF ᶜAMR IBN ᶜABASAH.

— 194 —

God extends His hand at night so that
He may accept the repentance of those
who indulge in wickedness
during the day.
God extends His hand during the day
so that He may accept the repentance of
those who indulge in wickedness
at night.
This will continue till the sun rises
in the west.

ḤADĪTH OF MUSLIM
ON THE AUTHORITY OF ABŪ MŪSĀ AL-ASHʿARĪ.

— 195 —

Those who remember God and those
who do not are as different from each
other as the living and the dead.

ḤADĪTH OF AL-BUKHĀRĪ AND MUSLIM
ON THE AUTHORITY OF ABŪ MŪSĀ AL-ASHʿARĪ.

— 196 —

According to Tamīm ad-Dārī,
the Prophet said,
'Well-wishing is faith.
Well-wishing is faith.
Well-wishing is faith.'
When asked towards whom, he replied,
'Towards God, His Messenger,
His Book,
the Muslim rulers and the
common people.'

ḤADĪTH OF MUSLIM.

— 197 —

Whenever the meal was concluded the
Prophet Muḥammad ﷺ would say,
'Praise be to Allah, in plenty,
in the best form and in abundance.
The praise, which we ourselves offer and
the praise which does not desert us, and
whose desire never leaves us and we do
not become indifferent to praise (of
God), O Our Lord.'

ḤADĪTH OF AL-BUKHĀRĪ
ON THE AUTHORITY OF ABŪ UMĀMAH.

— 198 —

God is bountiful and feels unhappy if He has to refuse to grant a wish. He feels embarrassed when a man holds out both his hands before Him, and He has to disappoint him by turning him away empty-handed.

ḤADĪTH OF ABŪ DĀWŪD AND AT-TIRMIDHĪ ON THE AUTHORITY OF SALMĀN AL-FĀRSĪ.

— 199 —

ʿAbdullāh ibn Masʿūd said, 'It is as if I see the Prophet Muḥammad ﷺ describing the life of one of the prophets,[1] who is assaulted by his people until the blood runs. He wipes the blood from his face and says, "O God, forgive my people for they know not what they do."'

ḤADĪTH OF BUKHĀRĪ AND MUSLIM.

1. THE ALLUSION IS PROBABLY MADE TO THE PROPHET NŪḤ (NOAH) عليه السلام.

— 200 —

O God, I seek divine guidance
so that I may remain steadfast
in what is just.
I seek divine guidance in order to be
firm in righteousness.
I seek divine guidance in the manner
that I express my gratitude
for Your favours
and worship with devotion.
I seek from You a tongue that speaks
the truth
and a heart which is pure
and clean.

ḤADĪTH OF AT-TIRMIDHĪ.

The Islamic Centre Publications

WOMAN BETWEEN ISLAM AND WESTERN SOCIETY

The status of woman in Islam is the same as that of man. Injunctions about honour and respect enjoined for one sex are enjoined equally for the other sex. So far as rights in this world and rewards in the Hereafter are concerned, there is no difference between the sexes. In the organization of daily living, both are equal participants and partners.

22 x 14.5 cm, 256 pages,

MUHAMMAD: THE PROPHET OF REVOLUTION

In making the Prophet Muhammad the greatest figure, and consequently one of the most resplendent landmarks in human history, God has bestowed his greatest favour on mankind. Whoever seeks guidance cannot fail to see him, for he stands out like a tower, a mountain on the horizon, radiating light like a beacon, beckoning all to the true path.

22 x 14.5 cm, 228 pages;

GOD-ORIENTED LIFE

The traditions—*sunnah*—of the Prophet Muhammad, upon whom be peace, and the lives of his companions and those closely associated with them, serve as a major source of religious enlightenment in theory and in practice. In that it culls from authentic sources the sayings and deeds of the Prophet and those inspired by him, it brings to us a complete and, above all, human picture of true Islamic behaviour.

22 x 14.5 cm, 186 pages;

ISLAM: THE VOICE OF HUMAN NATURE

Only God-centred religion is real and in harmony with man's nature. But this truth does not occur to him until the hour of crisis and peril is upon him. A man may have any religion, or any material props he chooses, but, in moments of real crisis, it is to God that he calls out for help. Any religion other than this will fail him in his hour of need, in the Hereafter, just as ordinary, everyday means of support so often do in moments of crisis in this world.
22 x 14.5 cm, 64 pages;

ISLAM: CREATOR OF THE MODERN AGE

Antiquity was an age of superstition: the present age is of science. Before reaching its present-day zenith, the modern, scientific age had to pass through three stages. The first was marked by the eradication of the superstitious mentality, the second saw the practical beginnings of scientific research; the third is the spectacular culmination of the scientific process in the second half of the twentieth century.

22 x 14.5 cm, 125 pages;

WOMAN IN ISLAMIC SHARI'AH

The contents of this book are as follows:

1. Qur'an and Hadith; 2. The Qualities of a Believing Woman; 3. Womanhood in Islam; 4. The Status of Woman; 5. Muslim Women; 6. The Rights of Husband and Wife; 7. Polygamy and Islam; 8. Dowry; 9. Hijab in Islam; 10. Concerning Divorce; 11. Success in Marriage

22 x 14.5 cm, 150 pages;

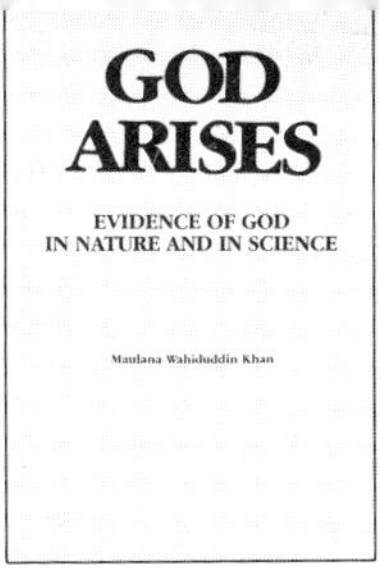

GOD ARISES

This book, the result of 30 years spent by the author in exhaustive research, attempts to present the basic teachings of religion in the light of modern knowledge and in a manner consistent with modern scientific method. After a thorough investigation of the subject, the writer has reached the conclusion that religious teachings are, academically, valid and as understandable and intellectually acceptable as any of the theories propounded by men of science.

22 × 14.5 cm, 271 pages;

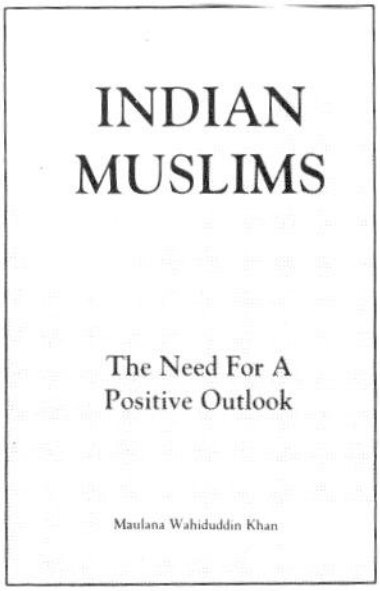

INDIAN MUSLIMS

Man must run the gauntlet of adversity in this life, for that is in the very nature of things. But repeated emphasis on the darker side of life, with no mention of brighter prospects ahead can lead only to discouragement, depression and inertia. The better way to find solutions to the problems besetting us would be to seek out and lay stress on whatever opportunities present themselves, so that those upon whom fortune has not smiled may feel encouraged to take the initiative in improving themselves and their lot in life.

22 × 14.5 cm, 192 pages;

ISLAM AS IT IS

In *Islam As It Is,* Maulana Wahiduddin Khan presents the fundamental teachings of Islam in a manner which will appeal directly to both general readers and students of Islam.

Simple and straightforward in style, *Islam As It Is* gives the reader an accurate and comprehensive picture of Islam—the true religion of submission to God.

22 × 14.5 cm, 114 pages;

THE ENCYCLOPAEDIA OF THE QUR'AN

The Encyclopaedia of the Qur'an is a unique work of reference which contains a mine of information both for family and educational use. It is extensively illustrated by photographs, maps and diagrams, many in full colour. It contains a wealth of information designed to give hours of reading, and spiritual enrichment to anyone interested in understanding the Qur'an.

Ideally suited for people of all ages and backgrounds, the *Encyclopaedia of the Qur'an* is an invaluable reference book for schools and colleges, students and teachers and for professionals and scholars. Even for relaxed browsing at home, the *Encyclopaedia of the Qur'an* will be found to contain a treasure trove of fascinating information affording hours of pleasurable reading. The Encyclopaedia is arranged in six well-illustrated sections: 1. Who's Who of the Qur'an, 2. Lands and Places of the Qur'an, 3: History of the Qur'an, 4. Understanding the Qur'an, 5. Studying the Qur'an, and 6. Ready Reference.

26×19.5cm, 400 pages. ISBN 81-85063-86-9
(Forthcoming, March 1996)

AL-RISALA BOOK CENTRE
1 Nizamuddin West Market, New Delhi 110013
Tel. 4611128 Fax: 91-11-4697333